Original title:
Hidden in the Hollow

Copyright © 2025 Creative Arts Management OÜ
All rights reserved.

Author: Harris Montgomery
ISBN HARDBACK: 978-1-80567-239-5
ISBN PAPERBACK: 978-1-80567-538-9

Shadows of the Forgotten Glen

In the glen where shadows play,
Squirrels wear hats in a comical way.
A rabbit steals carrots, but they can't see,
The giant snail slows down all to a tee.

Treetop chatter fills the air,
While owls wear glasses—what a funny pair!
The grass tickles toes, and the breeze gives a shove,
As laughter erupts from below and above.

Echoes from the Buried Path

On the path where the lost socks relax,
A raccoon reads comic books—what a knack!
With big glasses perched on a snout so cute,
It waves to the fox in a polka-dot suit.

The echoes of giggles bounce off the trees,
As ants hold a party with crumbs and some cheese.
A turtle breaks dance moves, slow but quite clear,
While the birds all chime in with a song we can hear.

Mysteries of the Shade-bound Thicket

In the thicket where whispers flit and flop,
A squirrel jokes that he'll never stop.
Raccoons in pajamas take a quick nap,
As butterflies gossip, "Did you see that trap?"

Mushrooms wear hats, and the ladybugs giggle,
As the shadows all jive in a silly wiggle.
A hedgehog plucks daisies, thinking he's cool,
While a badger constructs a miniature pool.

Ghosts of the Overgrown Clearings

In the clearing where tall weeds dance and sway,
Ghostly figures have a grand ole' play.
They swing from the branches, spirits untamed,
While a jester bird calls, "This is unframed!"

Mice in tuxedos waltz under the moon,
Their clever little moves make the shadows swoon.
With laughter like bubbles, their fun does not wane,
In this hidden delight, absolutely insane!

The Spun Webs of Nature's Conspiracy

In corners of chaos, spiders spin,
Their silk a plot for where bugs have been.
Each glistening thread, a laugh in disguise,
As breakfast arrives, much to their surprise.

Branches wave secrets, like whispers they share,
"Who'll trip on this root? Oh, do we dare?"
Squirrels giggle as nuts make a fall,
Nature conspires, and we're all part of the brawl.

Beneath the Green Canopy

Under the leaves, a party gets loud,
Frogs croak a tune, like they're so proud.
Turtles pull faces, spinning their shells,
While lizards jump in with their own hilarious yells.

The fun never stops, in the mossy nook,
A raccoon reads comics, oh what a crook!
An owl rolls its eyes, fed up with the noise,
As nature's mischief brings all the joys.

The Lurking Spirits of the Wood

With giggles and jigs, the spirits take flight,
They prank all the travelers all through the night.
A branch may just poke, or a twig give a snap,
Frisky old ghosts love a good cheeky yap.

"Who knew the oak could dance?" one did ask,
As fairies disguised took quite the small task.
Rustling leaves join in with glee and delight,
Creating a shindig till the morning light.

Echoes from the Secreted Glen

In the glen where secrets tickle the breeze,
Chirps trade jokes with the rustling trees.
A rabbit rolls over, laughing so loud,
While deer break out in a dance, so proud.

The shadows play tag, weaving in and out,
"Can you catch us?" they whisper, full of doubt.
From echoes around, laughter takes flight,
In this kooky nook, all feels just right.

Lattice of Unspoken Tales

In the tangled leaves, whispers play,
A squirrel debating the best nut today.
A snail on a journey, slow and grand,
Argues with shadows about the land.

A raccoon with tales of midnight feasts,
Tries to impress the gathering beasts.
While a frog croaks verses absurdly out loud,
His friends roll their eyes, a bemused crowd.

A breeze carries laughter from tree to tree,
As branches take bets on who might be free.
The air is alive with secrets so clear,
But not one is told, so they all persevere.

Beneath the canopy, stories unfold,
Of creatures and antics both daring and bold.
Join in the fun, but don't take a peek,
For in these tall tales, it's the laughter we seek.

Echoes in the Enigma

In shadows, where giggles softly collide,
A fox tells a tale with great pride.
He boasts of a chase that was frightfully fast,
While everyone knows that he always comes last.

A owl fluffs his feathers, wise and aloof,
But cracks jokes that often miss the proof.
The creatures all nod, though they don't understand,
As the hippo's loud laugh shakes the whole woodland.

Bathed in moonlight, the fireflies wail,
As rabbits engage in a wild bread trail.
The leap and the bounce, a dance so absurd,
Is met with confusion, yet not a harsh word.

Echoes of laughter envelop the night,
As critters share humor, their hearts feeling light.
In the grand web of life, it's all rather funny,
For who knew that laughter was so worth the money?

The Secret Life of Roots

Deep in the dirt, where the roots debate,
A worm claims he's really the dirtiest mate.
He laughs as the fungi roll their eyes,
Claiming his tales have no real surprise.

The thicket's deep voices start to conspire,
As tiny seeds giggle beside the fire.
The moles draw their plans for a grand underground,
While teasing the rabbits, who hop all around.

With whispers of fortune in every twist,
The roots pull each other to plan a tryst.
But oh! What a twist when the vines all collide,
Creating a mess that they cannot abide.

So down in the dark, with a ticklish cheer,
Each root takes a turn, making fun without fear.
In the earth's hidden chambers, mischief is rife,
For beneath the tall trees, there's a comical life.

Ghosts of the Forest Floor

Amidst the ferns where the shadows roam,
The ghosts of the forest find a new home.
They bicker and argue, what a silly lot,
Over the best way to spook a dot.

A leaf rustles gently, a joke takes its flight,
As the phantoms compete for a scare in the night.
The mushrooms stand guard, with their caps all aglow,
While the will-o'-the-wisps give a theatrical show.

They challenge the owls in a spook-off so grand,
With puns and strange ghouls that no one had planned.
A pumpkin rolls past, adding laughter to fright,
As the ghouls get the giggles while dancing in light.

So tread very softly on soft, ghostly ground,
Where echoes of laughter are plentiful and found.
For in this strange haunt, it's all joy and glee,
Among the lost spirits, as merry as can be.

Where the Light Meets the Gloom

In shadows where squirrels play,
And mushrooms dance in light of day.
The sunbeams poke, a funny sight,
As bunnies hop, avoiding fright.

Wiggly worms do wiggle through,
While hedgehogs search for lunch, it's true.
A fox with socks of vibrant hue,
Is lost on paths it thought it knew.

And if you trip on roots so sly,
You might just hear a laughing sigh.
For nature's jokes, they never cease,
As critters share a giggling peace.

So come enjoy this silly scene,
Where grass is wavy, bright, and green.
In the space where whimsy grows,
Lies laughter 'neath the leafy bows.

Buried Amongst Nature's Bounty

Beneath the leaves, a treasure trove,
Of acorns stacked and nuts that stove.
A chipmunk in a fluffy hat,
Is hiding snacks—imagine that!

Amongst the roots, the tangle tight,
A polka-dotted snail takes flight.
It dreams of racing leaves on high,
But only moves with gentle sighs.

Under the rocks, a toad does chant,
About its dreams to learn to dance.
While fireflies blink like jokes gone wild,
And ants march on, each little child.

So if you dig in dirt so fine,
You might just find a funny line.
With giggles lurking everywhere,
Nature's jesters fill the air!

The Lure of Unseen Paths

Upon a path not drawn on maps,
Where silly squirrels share their laughs.
A raccoon dreams of midnight snacks,
While wearing on its head some hacks.

The tall grass whispers secrets sweet,
About the ants that dance and greet.
A butterfly with socks so bright,
Flits tales of joy in morning light.

With every turn and twist on track,
You'll find a rabbit dressed in black.
It's lost, it says, but feels just right,
In this parade of pure delight.

So wander here, don't mind the wrong,
For whimsy sings its silly song.
These unseen paths, oh what a game,
Where every turn brings more of fame!

Mysteries of the Underbrush

Beneath the twigs and leaves so small,
A party brews both grand and tall.
The beetles dress in shiny wear,
As crickets jest without a care.

A badger plops with oh-so-much flair,
Pretending it belongs out there.
While spiders weave in funny shapes,
To trap the giggles from the crepes.

The shadows wiggle, twist, and twirl,
As plants do wink and soft winds whirl.
And if you peek, you might just see,
A hedgehog sipping tea with glee.

So take a stroll where bushes cheer,
And bring your friends, the fun is near.
In all the mysteries that bloom,
Lies laughter waiting in the room.

The Unseen World of Shadows

In the corners where echoes dwell,
Strange things dance, but none can tell.
A sock might giggle, a shoe might sigh,
While the dust bunnies leap and fly.

Cacti wear sunglasses, making a fuss,
While the old broom sings on the bus.
The toaster grins, in toasty delight,
As burnt toast flutters into the night.

Here, the chairs gossip, the curtains peek,
Whispering secrets of the hide-and-seek.
A coffee cup waves, the cats just yawn,
In this playful realm, the laughter's drawn.

So tiptoe softly, lend a quick ear,
In the unseen world, there's much to cheer.
For in shades and corners, whimsy ignites,
A funny charade of curious sights.

The Guardians of the Forgotten Brush

In gardens where the weeds do prance,
Brushes hold their own weird dance.
A paint-splattered cat dons a beret,
As it pirouettes the day away.

The old rake crackles, hosting a ball,
While the spade spins stories, loud and tall.
Worms wear tuxedos, worms wear shoes,
In this leafy realm, there's nothing to lose.

Amidst the petals, a gnome grins wide,
As hedges hum a sweet lullaby.
Forget not the faeries hiding near,
With mischief in minds and laughter to steer.

So next time you wander past that brush,
Remember the fun, the giggle, the hush.
For guardians of mischief live right in sight,
In that quirky world where shadows hold tight.

A Dance in the Quiet Shade

Underneath the arching trees,
Frogs in tuxedos croak with ease.
A ballet of bees buzz around,
While the trees sway with grace unbound.

With whispers of rustling leaves so clear,
The mushrooms waltz with giggles and cheer.
A snail in a top hat takes the floor,
As grasshoppers round up for more.

Lurking laughter in the cool night air,
Squirrels are prancing without a care.
A stylish ant leads the fun parade,
In shades where light and laughter invade.

So if you're quiet and linger near,
You'll catch the giggles, you'll hear the cheer.
In that dance of shadows, come join the spree,
Where the quiet shade holds a jolly decree.

The Secrets of Sun-dappled Glades

In the glades where sunlight breaks,
A squirrel tells tales of great mistakes.
The grass tickles toes in a happy spree,
While butterflies laugh at the buzzing bee.

A stony frog with a jester's cap,
Sings songs to the wind with a quirky clap.
The ferns share whispers of old-time lore,
While the daisies join in with a playful roar.

The gnarled old tree rolls its eyes in jest,
As shadows groove on a sunlit quest.
With every twirl, a giggle resounds,
In these sun-dappled spots where silliness bounds.

So parks your worries, let laughter commence,
For secrets live here, and they make no sense.
In every glade, a merry surprise,
Where giggles sprout and mischief lays ties.

Secrets Weaved in Green

A squirrel in a tiny hat,
Is plotting with a nearby cat.
They share their thoughts on acorn pies,
While giggling under leafy skies.

The mushrooms wink, the ferns will sway,
As critters dance the night away.
A rabbit with a bowtie bright,
Sings silly songs to the moonlight.

The thorns conspire, but oh, so meek,
With tales of cheese and hide-and-seek.
A chorus of chirps, a raucous cheer,
Invites mischief each time we're near.

Their secrets bloom in colors bold,
As tales of nuts and snacks are told.
An escapade in nature's play,
Where laughter grows and troubles sway.

The Silent Pulse of the Thicket

In shadows deep, sounds softly creep,
A fox in glasses takes a leap.
He writes his memoirs, very sly,
Of all the fruit that made him fly.

A bushy tail, it curls so fine,
While beavers sip on sparkling wine.
They toast to trees with silly grins,
And laugh at the whir of passing spins.

Amidst the ferns, a string band plays,
With crickets tapping out their praise.
The silent pulse of shenanigans,
Tick-tocking through the woodland plans.

With cackling laughs, the world they weave,
In thickets thick, where none believe.
A world where whimsy reigns so bright,
Till dawn appears to end the night.

Where Flora Hides its Secrets

In garden beds where daisies sprout,
A chatty worm spins tales about.
He claims to know the finest snacks,
While ladybugs don tiny hats.

The daisies giggle, the petals sway,
As sunbeams cast their golden play.
A rumor spreads like whispering breeze,
About the mage who talks to trees.

A flower with a twinkling grin,
Shares jokes with bees that buzz within.
They trade their puns and sips of dew,
Creating laughter, sweet and true.

In secret glades where giggles flow,
The flora spills what few can know.
Amongst the roots where stories flourish,
The humor blooms and hearts establish.

The Clouded Path of Whispers

Through misty trails of tangled fate,
A frog in shades begins to skate.
With every leap, he croaks a tune,
While clouds above dance the afternoon.

The gossip flows like bubbling brooks,
While snails read tales from nature's books.
Inside a thicket, secrets blend,
As laughter rings around each bend.

A bashful hedgehog writes a play,
About the antics of his day.
He casts his friends as trees and bees,
That sway and flutter in the breeze.

In this clouded maze, so full of cheer,
The whispers echo, loud and clear.
Where every creature's jest and song,
For in this thicket, they all belong.

Enclaves of Forgotten Dreams

In a nook where squeaky mice play,
Old toys whisper, 'Come out and stay.'
A candy wrapper waves hello,
While dust bunnies dance to and fro.

Beneath the bed, a sock takes flight,
It claims it's catching dreams tonight.
A teddy bear strums on a string,
As forgotten thoughts begin to sing.

The closet groans with secrets bold,
Jackets laughing, tales retold.
In this space of giggles and glee,
Lost fantasies roam, wild and free.

So tiptoe in, your heart must race,
With each peek, you'll find a trace.
In this whimsical, playful tease,
Where imagination finds its keys.

The Hidden Echos of Earth

Deep in the ground, where worms convene,
A misplaced shoe declares it's seen.
Echoes of laughter from grasshopper bands,
Tickle the toes of the wandering hands.

Rocks whisper, 'Hey, we've something to share,'
As ants march past without a care.
A gopher remarks, 'This spot is prime,'
With secret stories trapped in slime.

Roots entwined, they conspire and plot,
Making the ground a dizzying lot.
Oh, the mischief that soil can bring,
With roots that tickle and stones that sing!

So if you kneel and listen real close,
You might hear the earth giggle and boast.
In this realm where the wild things cheer,
Nature's humor is crystal clear.

Where Mystery Lingers

A curtain of vines, a shadowed veil,
Where whispers of frights tell a funny tale.
A ghost with a grin and a slight wobble,
Turns fright into laughter, what a noble bobble!

Behind a bush, a frog plays the flute,
While squirrels in hats dance in pursuit.
Bubbles of giggles float in the air,
While secrets and starlight twirl everywhere.

The path meanders, but don't be misled,
You may trip on a toe or fall on your head!
Yet every tumble brings chuckles anew,
Where the bizarre blooms, and laughter ensues.

So venture forth into the unknown,
With a spirit of fun that's brightly shown.
In this realm where the oddities shine,
Every shadow holds a joke divine.

Legends Beneath the Old Oak

Under branches where whispers creep,
Lies a tale that makes even owls leap.
A gnome with a beard bids you to stay,
And shares that rain dances have humorous sway.

The acorns debate on the best nutty puns,
While squirrels throw jokes like fetching runs.
The roots snicker with wisdom so grand,
As they plot mischief across the land.

There's a ticklish breeze that ruffles the leaves,
Confetti of laughter that no one believes.
A raccoon plays chess with a sneaky old crow,
In a world where antics perpetually flow.

So sit by the oak, it's a riotous place,
Where each crinkled leaf hides a smiley face.
In this haven where legends abound,
Funny fables eternally found.

Beneath the Veil of Leaves

A squirrel's dance, a sight to see,
Chasing shadows, wild and free.
A ninja acorn, swift and sly,
With one brave leap, it bids goodbye.

Mice have meetings, tea in the sun,
Whispering secrets, having some fun.
A dandelion, puffed up with pride,
Sways in the breeze, a pompous guide.

Laughter echoes where shadows creep,
A wily fox has no time for sleep.
He's plotting paths for tricks to play,
While butterflies laugh and flit away.

Under the bark, a party's loud,
With crickets crooning to the crowd.
Next to a slug, the snail's on a roll,
Living it up in nature's coal.

The Quiet Nest of Dreams

In a cozy nook where the sunlight lingers,
A mouse in slippers waves all his fingers.
He'll bake a cake of crumbly delight,
While dreaming of cheese, oh what a sight!

A sleepy owl in a robe of grey,
Hoots out puns at the end of the day.
With laughter swirling through leaves and boughs,
Nature's jesters take their bows.

A powered-up beetle, racing around,
Thinks he's a rocket, oh what a sound!
He zooms past shadows with vigor and glee,
Making rivals jealous as can be.

Little frogs holding comedy shows,
Ribbiting jokes while the river flows.
They leap and they spring, full of fun,
The night's laughter has just begun!

Lurking in the Verdant Silence

A snail in sunglasses, cool as can be,
Waves to a ladybug sipping its tea.
They giggle at petals that tickle their toes,
In an evening filled with whimsical prose.

Kittens play chess with shadows of trees,
Strategizing moves over rustling leaves.
The game's a bit slow, but hearts play on,
With mouses as pawns till the break of dawn.

A worm in a hat tells tales of the past,
About days when the rain fell hard and fast.
With laughter and tales twirling in air,
Their roots stretch deeper, no room for despair.

Under the stars, frogs croon out a tune,
Echoing whispers of an old silver moon.
They leap with delight, to a rhythm so bright,
In the emerald hush, everything's light.

The Forgotten Cradle of Nature

Amidst the weeds, a wise old tree,
Cracks jokes with the breeze, just wait and see!
Its branches wave like hands in the air,
Singing a tune in a voice so rare.

A hedgehog host is bustling about,
Serving up meals with a cheeky shout.
"More worms, more slugs!" he cheers with a grin,
As critters in bow ties start to come in.

Ladybugs wear spots of red and black,
While butterflies join for a welcome snack.
They laugh and they twirl under foliage bright,
In this shelter where joy takes flight.

At dusk, the stars sprinkle jokes from above,
While critters revel in mystical love.
Every ripple and rustle, a playful tease,
All in the cradle where wonders never cease.

Beneath the Surface of Solitude

In a cozy nook where the shadows play,
A cat wears a cape and thinks it's a sleigh.
A squirrel in disguise throws acorns with flair,
While gossiping mushrooms plot mischief and scare.

A puddle reflects all the secrets it keeps,
As a frog in a top hat rudely interrupts sleeps.
With giggles and snorts, the moon winks above,
As crickets decide it's a night full of love.

A snail dreams of races, absurd and quite slow,
While a fern shakes its fronds, "Join the fun, don't be low!"
The ants march in lines—oh, what a fine sight!
Dressed up for a fiesta under starlit delight.

So if you seek laughter, just peek at the trees,
Where whispers of nonsense dance lightly on breeze.
In the corners of quiet, hilarity waits,
With creatures and capers that brighten the fates.

Enigma of the Wild Understory

In the tangled weeds where the odd things grow,
A hedgehog in socks puts on quite a show.
With a jive and a twist, he grooves with the leaves,
While grasshoppers giggle and dance in their sleeves.

A fox on the prowl wears a hat made of cheese,
Declaring, "It's fashion! Every creature agrees!"
The woodpecker chuckles with rhythmic delight,
Pecking out laughter in the pale moonlight.

An owl with a monocle reads nightly news,
While badgers play cards with the slyest of cues.
An empty log serves as a stage for a play,
As the actors in feathers steal scenes, without sway.

Underground chatter brings stories to light,
A worm writes a novel by the glow of the night.
In the underbrush, brilliance and whimsy hold sway,
In the jungle of joy, come and frolic this way.

The Soft Breath of Seclusion

In a secret grove where the breezes can tease,
A rabbit in glasses sips tea from a freeze.
With thoughts quite profound and a biscuit or two,
He ponders the universe, dreams he can view.

A turtle with swagger races time on a clock,
While shadows of flowers dance round like a flock.
Each petal declares, "We're the stars of this show!"
While the brook whispers jokes as it trickles below.

A lone crone of the night spins tales in the dark,
With fireflies buzzing, they light up the park.
A raccoon, quite charming, collects twinkling things,
As the stars in the sky stick on their bright blings.

In this secretive realm, chuckles reign free,
Where snickers and giggles join in harmony.
From laughter to whispers, the joy intertwines,
In a space of seclusion, where humor just shines.

Bound by the Thicket's Embrace

In a thicket so thick, where the wild things conspire,
A parrot tells jokes that could light up a fire.
With feathers so bright, he caws with delight,
As shenanigans spark in the cool of the night.

An otter in boots takes a slide down the brook,
While the reeds play a duet, as if from a book.
Their harmonies blend with a raucous galore,
As frogs leap with laughter, demanding encore.

A mole with a top hat pulls tricks from a sack,
While the grasses all giggle behind his own back.
The chatter of critters creates quite the sound,
As the mischief of nature flits all around.

In this playful realm where the silly run free,
Find joy in the jests that hide under the tree.
For in every nook and the crannies so snug,
Lies laughter galore, like a warm, fuzzy hug.

The Allure of Shadows Unveiled

In the nook where lost toys dwell,
A garden gnome begins to yell.
He thinks he's king of this small spot,
While bees buzz loudly, 'Hey, you're not!'

With squirrels dancing on the lawn,
He shakes his fist at early dawn.
A secret pact with plants they make,
To hold a race - oh what a cake!

Their laughter echoes through the air,
As laughter blends with sunny glare.
The gnome, bemused, can only cheer,
For shadows dance and bring good cheer.

So if you find a hidden nook,
Where shadows smile, just take a look.
You might just spot a new friend there,
With wise old tales beyond compare.

The Lament of the Overgrown

In tangled weeds where daisies thrive,
A chubby snail begins to dive.
He sighs for space to wiggle free,
But all he sees is greenery!

The flowers giggle in a breeze,
While he just wants a bit of ease.
But vines entwine, they plot and scheme,
To hide the snail's escape, it seems.

With every turn, he bumps and bounces,
Amidst the shrubs where mischief pounces.
He dreams of paths serene and clear,
Not tripping over roots, oh dear!

Yet in this mess, he finds delight,
With worms to chat and stars at night.
For who needs rooms or tidy space,
When laughter fills this blurry place?

In the Company of Silent Watchers

Beneath the trees, in mossy rows,
Foxes snooze as nobody knows.
With wise old owls perched up so high,
They give a wink — they can't deny!

A rabbit hops, quite unaware,
That shadows breathe a curious air.
The whispers float as tales unfold,
Of midnight dances, brave and bold.

They giggle soft and plan their pranks,
As crickets join in, forming ranks.
With sparkly eyes, the night rolls on,
A party blooms, till breaks of dawn.

And though they look like rocks or trees,
In secret, they are laughing, see?
For every glance, they raise a cheer,
For friendships made, both far and near.

Enfolded in the Moss's Caress

Where soft green pillows hug the ground,
A sleepy hedgehog curls around.
He dreams of cheese and bonnie fields,
While Nature spins her playful shields.

The riddles float like gentle mist,
With whispers of a squirrel's tryst.
A leaf confetti drops in play,
As mushrooms giggle all the day.

"Oh, what a life!" the hedgehog sighs,
As birds above fling down their cries.
In mossy blankets, jokes are stitched,
As laughter within nature's switched.

So if you wander where it's green,
Find the critters that laugh unseen.
For in the laughter, secret blends,
And joy abounds where stillness ends.

Nature's Veil of Solitude

In a forest where gnomes love to play,
A squirrel miscounts its acorn display.
The fox wears a hat, it's quite the sight,
While dancing with shadows, they party all night.

A bear with a bow tie sits sipping tea,
He invites all his friends, including a bee.
They laugh at the trees that wiggle and sway,
But giggles erupt when they all run away!

A turtle sings songs of a slow-moving tune,
While rabbits keep leapfrogging under the moon.
Each critter adds jest to the nature parade,
While the old owl snoozes, unfazed and unpaged.

So if you tread softly, and peek with a grin,
You may spot the odd group where the fun's tucked in.
In a world where the creatures all frolic and jive,
It's a chuckle-filled tale that keeps joy alive.

Murmurs from the Green Abyss

The trees whisper gossip, so juicy and bold,
About a raccoon who's become quite old.
He wears mismatched socks and a hat on his head,
Claiming he's chic while snoozing in bed.

In the depths of the brush, where the odd things dwell,
A hedgehog recites jokes about snail in a shell.
He rolls on the ground, giggling with glee,
Till he bumps into mushrooms that shout, "Can't see!"

A mouse in pink slippers skates over the dirt,
While a llama in sneakers yells, "Hey, you'll get hurt!"
They hold a parade with balloons made of grass,
And the butterflies flutter, all fancy and crass.

With laughter echoing through the thick green maze,
The critters all dance in a wacky, wild daze.
In this zany realm of mischief and cheer,
Every shadow holds laughter, oh dear, oh dear!

In the Heart of the Thicket

The thicket's a stage for a bold little show,
Where ladybugs twirl, and snails steal the glow.
A frog in a tux sings a croaky old tune,
While crickets are clapping beneath the round moon.

A hedgehog conducts with a stick made of twigs,
Directing the dance of the wobbling pigs.
They stumble and hiccup, a comedic affair,
While fireflies flicker and light up the air.

A raccoon on a skateboard glides fast by a tree,
He crashes and laughs, it's a sight to see!
The chattering squirrels all fall in a heap,
As the owls above watch, their eyes half-asleep.

In this bustling nook full of giggles and cheer,
Nature's a circus, with laughter sincere.
So join in the fun if you dare tread too near,
You'll leave with a smile and a tickle of cheer!

The Understory's Silent Secrets

Beneath leafy canopies, mischief abounds,
Where whispers of laughter escape from the grounds.
A gopher in goggles digs with such flair,
While rabbits are plotting their next big affair.

A deer with a bow and a quiver of snacks,
Calls out to the fox, "Let's launch some attacks!"
They race through the bushes in outrageous style,
Till they trip on a root, and it's giggles awhile.

The mushrooms are chatting, all silly and bright,
Debating which critter's the funniest sight.
With jests about turtles who wish they could fly,
And wrap-around vines that dance and comply.

So should you explore where the secrets are spun,
Wear a smile, hold tight, for the laughter's begun.
In the understory's world, surprises never cease,
With critters who cherish their moments of peace.

The Gathering of Secrets

In the crook of the pine, they meet,
Squirrels prance with a drumbeat.
A rabbit named Larry spills the beans,
On sneaky raccoons and their schemes.

Chasing shadows and lost old nuts,
They joke about foxes and their butts.
A turtle named Bob rolls on the ground,
Laughing at secrets that seem so profound.

The wise old owl rolls his eyes,
While a hedgehog spins clever lies.
Each giggle is soft, yet it stirs the air,
Turned by the wind with a ticklish flair.

As night falls and the stars play peek,
They promise to meet every week.
With laughter echoing through the glen,
They'll gather again, and the fun won't end.

Where the Ferns Whisper Softly

Where the ferns twist and dance in glee,
A family of owls has a cup of tea.
Sippin' and spillin' their latest news,
About chatting mice and their tiny shoes.

A chipmunk with style, so bold and grand,
Struts his stuff like he's in a band.
With each little hop, the ground starts to shake,
Even the stones join in for a quake!

The fireflies blink, playing a game,
While shadows join in, without any shame.
Hiccups of laughter surge through the night,
As leaf tickles spread pure delight.

And when the moon shines down its bright rays,
The critters all share their mischievous ways.
In ferny corners where tales never fold,
Laughter spices secrets, new and old.

The Hushed Chronicles of the Thicket

In the thicket so dense and dark,
A raccoon named Clyde found a snack-sized spark.
His buddies all laughed, what a sight to see,
As he juggled acorns with glee and glee.

The hedgehog rolled by with a twisty plan,
To start a rumor about the little man.
A rumor so wild and completely absurd,
That even the crows gasped and blurred.

Blushing flowers giggle, overhearing it all,
Trying to stifle the giggles that call.
Swaying with mirth, they secretly bloom,
As whispers of folly fill up the room.

With every tall tale, a new laugh occurs,
Woven together like raindrops and spurs.
In the thicket, where fun is the lore,
Secrets are penned, then shared, and explored.

Under the Boughs of Secrecy

Under the boughs where the shadows play,
An ant and a snail plan a grand soirée.
Inviting a worm with a top hat and cane,
For music that wobbles like dancing in rain.

The grass whispers softly with tales so weird,
About a butterfly, all brightly adorned.
Spreading stories with delicate flight,
She flutters and twirls, a marvelous sight.

The slugs slip and slide, making quite a show,
While the crickets chirp a rhythmic flow.
'What's the punchline?' a beetle inquires,
As laughter spreads out like twinkling fires.

So under these boughs, the secrets unfold,
In chuckles and giggles, the tales are retold.
From acorns to berries, they dearly convene,
Creating a ruckus that's sweet and serene.

The Quietude of the Concealed Hollow

In the woods where whispers tease,
A squirrel sneezes, oh what a breeze!
The rabbit laughs, the deer can't see,
They trip on roots, oh glee, oh glee!

A hedgehog snores by the old oak tree,
Dreaming of donuts awfully free.
The owls hoot jokes, a secret pass,
Their feathers ruffle, oh what a gas!

The chipmunk juggles acorns in place,
With a grin so wide, it's pure disgrace.
A plump raccoon joins in the fun,
Under the stars, till the night is done.

And if you venture, just take a peek,
You'll find the pranks that make critters squeak.
Laughter echoes, a mischievous band,
In the secret glade, that is simply grand!

Secrets in the Underwood

A tangle of tales in the loamy ground,
Where mushrooms dance, and critters abound.
A fox tells jokes about his own tail,
While the ants in lines march off on a trail.

The badger makes tea with a flower bloom,
And mammoth laughs cause a sweet perfume.
The fireflies flicker, gossiping bright,
About the moon's wig made of starlight.

A sneaky raccoon with a twinkle in eye,
Swipes a snack and waves goodbye.
The bushes rustle, a giggle and sigh,
As the plucky birds pass with a cheerful cry.

So if you listen, you might just hear,
A symphony of mischief, oh bring it near!
The secrets that peek in the leafy din,
Will tickle your heart and make you grin!

The Enchanted Depths of the Wood

In an oak's embrace, a gnome will poke,
With a wink and a nod, he'll tell a joke.
The fairies twirl on a dandelion seed,
Sprinkling laughter, oh what fun, indeed!

The mice juggle nuts, as the badgers cheer,
While the turtles spin tales of yesteryear.
A raccoon snores with crumbs on his face,
Dreaming of cookies, what a fine place!

A wise old owl with spectacles thick,
Tells a riddle, oh what a trick!
Squeaky shoes rustle as critters convene,
For a party that's pure, a jovial scene.

At dusk, when shadows flit and play,
They hoot and they holler, come join the fray!
For in the depths where the wild things tread,
A treasure of laughter is happily spread!

Between the Twining Vines

Where vines twist and curl in a playful dance,
Squirrels chase dreams, give laughter a chance.
A hedgehog rolls down a hillside so steep,
Giggles abound, their joy is deep.

The insects hum tunes, a charming hum,
As the mushrooms sway, they tap and drum.
Caterpillars form a conga line,
With butterflies twirling, it's quite divine!

A raccoon in shades, cool as can be,
Sips berry juice with flair and glee.
The lizards laugh, hanging out on a leaf,
Sharing tall tales, what a great relief!

So wander the path, let your spirit soar,
In the whimsy of vines, there's always more.
Each rustle and giggle is a map to find,
The laughter that lives where the heart is blind!

Beneath the Earth's Tender Shroud

Underneath the leafy ground,
A pile of socks is what I found.
Worms in hats hold secret talks,
While ants march in with tiny clocks.

Mice trade cheese for great ideas,
While moles sip tea and swap their fears.
Rabbits giggle at the sight,
Of grasshoppers that dance at night.

The roots above wear silly shoes,
And snails recite their terrible news.
The earth just laughs, it's quite a scene,
Underneath that gentle green.

Lost in the Embrace of Greenery

A squirrel forgot where acorns lay,
He danced around in a silly way.
The bushes chuckled, the trees swayed,
As he searched for his snack, so dismayed.

The vines were tangled, what a plight,
He tried to climb but took a flight!
With leafy hands they pulled him down,
As laughter echoed all around.

A hedgehog rolled by, with style so neat,
He offered help, but got stuck, oh sweet!
Together they hatched a plan so grand,
While the greens chuckled at their band.

Finally free, they dashed away,
Finding nuts and mushrooms on their way.
"Next time," they said, "we'll read the signs,
Before delving deep in tangled vines!"

Whispers of the Sunken Grove

In a grove where shadows flit,
Trees gossip and squirrels knit.
Goblins play with mushrooms round,
As giggles echo in the ground.

A fox in boots tells tales so tall,
Of woolly sheep who couldn't crawl.
A sneezy bear can't catch a fish,
Which sparks a wish for something squished.

The pond reflects a winking frog,
Who juggles flies in a thick fog.
The whispers twist, they bubble and pop,
As creatures toss their worries and hop.

Secrets Beneath the Canopy

Birds with hats sit in a row,
Chirping gossip nice and slow.
Under leaves, a party brews,
Toasting nuts and fancy shoes.

Trees wear coats of vibrant hue,
While raccoons plot what they might do.
They'll raid the picnic, that's the plan,
As the wind hums a jaunty span.

A wise old owl lends an ear,
To all the laughter he can hear.
"Keep it down!" they plea with glee,
But mischief sweeps like a wild spree.

So beneath the leaves, they plot and scheme,
In nature's arms, there's room to dream.
With silly antics, they all play,
In the heart of the trees, they lose the day.

The Veiled Symphony of the Wild

Amidst the trees, a tune so bright,
A squirrel dance, quite the sight!
With acorns tossed in rhythmic flair,
A furry band without a care.

They twirl and leap, no time to nap,
Creating music, a nutty clap!
While birds join in with high-pitched glee,
Nature's concert, wild and free.

But who will pay this furry crew?
Perhaps a raccoon in a tutu?
With clumsy paws, he takes the stage,
Making everyone laugh in rage.

So join the game, don't sit and stare,
For laughter hides within the air.
In woodland grooves, we find our play,
Where joy is found in every sway.

Secrets Nestled in Twilight

Twilight whispers with a gentle sigh,
A gnome sneezes, oh my oh my!
His tiny hat fell in a splash,
As fireflies giggle, flickering fast!

The mossy rocks, they share their lore,
Of woodland secrets, and much more.
A frog's croak echoes, making news,
A fish in moonlit ponds just snooze.

The wise old owl can't help but chuckle,
Watching rabbits play in a huddle.
But as they hop, they trip on roots,
Falling down in silly suits!

So if you wander where stories bloom,
Listen close for laughter's tune.
In twilight's grasp, the fun ignites,
With every secret, joy ignites!

The Sanctuary of Overhanging Branches

Under branches, the path winds tight,
With shadows dancing, a joyful sight.
A hedgehog grins, he knows a trick,
He rolls away, oh what a flick!

Beneath a leaf, a turtle sings,
About the joy that nature brings.
While bunnies hop, they start to race,
Chasing their tails in a wild embrace.

A faint noise echoes, what could it be?
A raccoon munching on a berry spree!
With sticky paws, he poses so grand,
A king of snacks in this vast land!

So wander in where laughter hides,
In leafy nooks, where fun abides.
The sanctuary smiles, let's take part,
In this woodland realm, it fills the heart!

Whispers of the Untraveled Way

In a lane less walked, where mischief roams,
Lies a patch where silly gnomes.
With hats askew and shoelaces tied,
They plan a game, a grand joyride!

A raccoon leans in with a secret plan,
To steal some snacks with a feline clan.
But kittens' pounces turn into play,
As laughter bubbles in a delightful way!

The sun dips low, the fireflies glow,
These merry creatures put on a show.
With playful pranks and silly tricks,
They keep us smiling, avoiding the fix.

So venture forth where whispers tease,
In lighthearted paths, feel the breeze.
With every step, find joy in play,
In this realm where laughter stays!

Lurking Beneath the Leafy Veil

Beneath the leaves, just out of sight,
A squirrel plays tricks, oh what a fright!
He chatters and chuckles, then darts away,
With acorns in hand, he's won the day.

A raccoon grins, with paws all sticky,
Stealing snacks, oh isn't that tricky?
He winks at the birds, perched high on a tree,
While plotting a heist, he's as sly as can be.

Mice dance in shadows, they think it's a game,
Wearing tiny hats, they're all the same.
They giggle and wiggle, it's a wild charade,
With squeaks and with squeals, their plans are displayed.

So if you wander and hear a strange sound,
Know that mischief is lurking around!
Nature's a circus, oh what a delight,
Where laughter and chaos take flight every night.

Tales from the Twilight Brush

In twilight's brush, where shadows play,
A hedgehog tumbles, no care for the way.
He rolls like a tumbleweed, round and around,
With giggles of crickets, his laughter is found.

Frogs host a concert, they croak and they leap,
In synchronized stages, no need for sleep.
While owls in their wisdom try to keep time,
They hoot in confusion, not missing a rhyme.

The stars above twinkle with glee,
As fireflies twirl like they own the decree.
A dance-off erupts, with critters so spry,
As the moon watches over, a proud, glowing eye.

So gather your giggles beneath the night's dome,
For nature's a jester that feels just like home!
Every chuckle and chirp, a story to tell,
In the twilight brush, all's ill at ease but swell.

The Lurking Secrets of Nature

Down in the flowers, beneath the bright bloom,
An ant takes a selfie, in nature's big room.
With friends all around, he strikes a proud pose,
While bees buzz in chorus, with smiles on their nose.

A fox in the thicket wears poor-looking socks,
Trying to blend in, but he's tricked by the clocks.
He trips on a root, oh what a display,
As rabbits around him all laugh and then sway!

The wind plays the harp, with its breezy embrace,
Tickling the leaves in a whimsical race.
While turtles in shell-backs lounge on a log,
They share all their secrets, with every chattering frog.

So venture outside, in this playful parade,
Nature's a jester, where joy won't degrade.
With giggles and grins, let your heart feel the thrill,
For in every odd corner, there's laughter to fill.

Enigmas in the Secreted Enclave

In a nook of the woods, where giggles abound,
A gopher holds parties, quite underground.
With confetti of dirt and a dance made of cheer,
He hosts wild soirées, with a wink and a sneer.

The owls drop by, all dressed up for the show,
With monocles firmly, and a dash of debonair flow.
They hoot out the tunes, oh so suave and refined,
While the chipmunks do flips, impressive and blind.

The streams sing of secrets, in bubbly delight,
As frogs wear their crowns, in the glow of moonlight.
With a splash and a dance, they flaunt their best moves,
And mischief and magic are what nature proves.

So come take a look, through the leaves and the trees,
Where enigma and laughter swirl fresh with the breeze.
In this enclave of fun, where spirits can leap,
Unravel the riddles, and sow joy that's deep.

The Gloomy Embrace of Roots

Beneath the ground, a rooted jest,
Where socks and shoes have taken rest.
A phantom dance of dirt and grime,
The rhubarb giggles at the thyme.

Moles wear hats and throw a bash,
While rabbits cook up their sweet stash.
The straggling vines join in the game,
And every turn, it's just the same!

A tangle here, a twisty shout,
As gnomes emerge, all filled with doubt.
With barbecues that start to flare,
It's just a plunge, we haven't a care!

And if you peek beneath the leaves,
You'll find the secrets that it weaves.
So grab your spade, come take a seat,
For laughter bubbles 'neath your feet!

Chasing Shadows in the Green Mist

In the fog where shadows play,
Squirrels plotting mischief's way.
They steal your snacks and giggle loud,
While dancing in their leafy shroud.

A toad in flippers waddles near,
Wearing glasses, sipping beer.
With every leap, a splashing score,
Making puddles, that's the lore!

Brambles whisper jokes, so sly,
While fireflies zoom and flutter by.
A game of hide and seek ensues,
With every peep, they shift their hues.

So chase the shadows, don't be shy,
Where laughter sparkles, oh my, oh my!
The misty greens hold quirky throngs,
A raucous tune of nature's songs!

The Timeless Whispers of the Glen

In the glen where giggles roam,
A feathered mime has found a home.
With quirks and quirks that make you snort,
The breeze conducts a funny sort.

An acorn fell and made a scene,
A squirrel dressed in denim jeans.
With little boots and stylish flair,
It shimmies by without a care!

A wise old fox with specs so round,
Reads poetry to crickets' sound.
The trees nod softly, laugh away,
As nature joins the grand ballet!

So twirl in laughter, spin in light,
The timeless whispers, pure delight.
Return to see what waits anew,
In every nook, a giggle too!

The Eclipsed Light of Secret Worlds

In the corners where the wild things hide,
A disco ball spins with playful pride.
The mushrooms sway to her sweet tunes,
While raccoons share their silly loons.

The fireflies glow in awkward sync,
Their lights a wink, a giggly link.
In shadows deep, a rabble rouse,
As owls wear frowns but still espouse.

A lizard sings with a rockstar flair,
Perched on a log, without a care.
While frogs in chorus croak so loud,
This secret world is quite the crowd!

So join the fun, don't drift away,
In the eclipsed light where critters play.
For every laugh a treasure holds,
Within the tales that nature molds!

Secrets of the Dusky Dell

In a dell where secrets creep,
A squirrel whispers, cannot sleep.
He's got a nut that's way too big,
Now it's stuck, oh what a gig!

A bunny hops with quite a flair,
Wearing glasses, reading there!
Each page flipped, a giggle spills,
His book: 'How to Run from Chills!'

A hedgehog rolls, a tiny ball,
But wobbles like he's drunk at all.
He bumps a tree, what a loud thud,
And falls right in, now that's real mud!

The badger's got a dance routine,
But twirls too fast, he's quite unseen.
He tries to glide, oh what a sight,
Tripped by roots, he took a flight!

Nature's Quiet Enigma

A wise old owl sits perched and stares,
Deciphers riddles with avocado pairs.
He's plotting schemes, no doubt about,
For midnight snacks he'll dance around.

The flowers giggle, sway in glee,
As bees buzz past, oh can't you see?
They steal their pollen, what a ruckus!
The daisies shout, 'Now that's just dumb us!'

A frog croaks out his fanciest tune,
Thinking he'll charm the clouds and moon.
But all that croaking, it drives them mad,
And now the stars are just plain sad!

A chipmunk juggles acorns, quite absurd,
While slipping on comical word after word.
He falls on his tail, what a funny sight,
Bumbling around under the pale moonlight!

The Silent Song of the Enclosed Glade

In the glade where shadows glance,
A turtle's having a slow dance.
With hips so wide, and moves so grand,
He's leading a fox in a wobbly band.

A lizard struts in a flashy vest,
Remarking how he's simply the best.
But trips on leaves, oh what a joke,
Flashing his colors, oh what a bloke!

The crickets play a silly tune,
While bugs breakdance under the moon.
Each stomp and hop, a comical cheer,
As mouse breaks out with an awkward sphere.

But nature knows how to keep it light,
With chuckles kept well out of sight.
In this glade, all creatures delight,
Crafting laughter till the morning light!

Shadows in the Whispering Wood

Deep within the woods so sly,
A shadow laughs, oh my oh my!
It tickles trees and makes them sway,
While squirrels ponder if they can play!

A moose with shoes sings out a tune,
Waltzing with a raccoon by the moon.
They tap their feet on logs so round,
Creating beats that shake the ground!

A snail slides in with pearls so bright,
Claiming to sparkle all night long, what a sight!
But slips on dew, lands in a gloop,
Now he's part of the midnight loop!

With laughter echoing through the trees,
The shadows sway with the playful breeze.
In this wood where silliness hides,
Joy and giggles will forever abide!

Where Stillness Breeds Mystery

In the quiet grove, a squirrel talks,
To a clammy toad in oversized socks.
A fox in a hat winks at the trees,
While a snail takes a ride on a gentle breeze.

The shadows chuckle, the owls roll their eyes,
As the daisies gossip, revealing some lies.
Behind leafy curtains, a raccoon prepares,
To start a parade, with feathers and flares.

Mushrooms tap dance in a delightful show,
While crickets chirp out a tune full of glow.
Every branch seems to strut, not a creature aloof,
In this comedy hall, the trees raise the roof.

So gather 'round friends, and bring your best cheer,
For laughter's the language that all will hold dear.
In the stillness, mischief is surely at play,
As giggles and snorts dance the night away.

The Unraveled Tales of Nature

A wise old owl once wore a cape,
Chasing his dreams on a fruit crate.
The ants held a council, oh what a sight,
Debating if fruit flies could ever take flight.

A bear painted stripes, just for the fun,
He said, 'I'm a zebra, now isn't that pun?'
While turtles debated the speed of their race,
And a rabbit declared, 'I need my own space!'

A wisecracking crow stole the sun's golden glare,
While flowers all giggled, twirling in air.
The wind told a story, unflattering yet bright,
Of a snail who convinced the moon to take flight.

So let's toast to trees with their funny old bark,
To the laughter of leaves, igniting a spark.
For nature's a tapestry woven with glee,
Where stories unravel, wild and free.

Lost Legends in the Thicket

In the thicket, a legend was born at dawn,
Of a hedgehog who thought he was a fawn.
With a crown made of leaves, he swaggered with pride,
While a badger called, 'Mate, there's no need to hide!'

A party ensued with mushrooms for cake,
As beetles and bugs danced near a warm lake.
A parrot recited tall tales of old,
While a bumblebee dreamt of wonders untold.

The bushes were alive with snickers and schmooze,
As vines played tricks, and the thicket would snooze.
Said the fox in the bush, 'We're legends, you see,
In a world of absurdity, let it be free!'

So if you wander, just look for the fun,
In the whispers of leaves, where all laughs run.
For lost tales emerge in the dappled sun's flare,
A triumph of humor fills the thick, fragrant air.

Traces of the Hidden Realm

In a nook by the brook, a rabbit did boast,
Of a party with gnomes and the local ghost.
With cupcakes and giggles, they danced 'til the morn,
While a cat in a bow tie played tunes with a horn.

The trees held their breath, as secrets were spun,
About how the hedgehogs had all tried to run.
Yet they tripped on their quills, what a sight to behold,
The laughter erupted, worth more than gold.

A beetle dressed sharply, a monocle set,
Debated with butterflies whom he called 'pet'.
Said, 'Let's leave the worries where daisies poke fun,
For the traces of joy are forever begun.'

So venture on paths where nonsense blooms bright,
In the corners of nature where whimsy takes flight.
For the hidden realm waits for laughter and play,
In the traces of life that brighten the day.

Whispers Beneath the Canopy

Beneath the leaves, a squirrel grins,
While gossip flows, the mischief spins.
A deer tells tales of food buffet,
With snacks shoved in from yesterday!

The owls are hooting, but watch them blink,
Their secrets spilled with every wink.
The frogs in chorus croak in jest,
A swampy song; they think they're best!

A rabbit raves about a race,
Claims he's won a marathon space.
But we've all seen his sneaky feet,
He zigzagged past - oh what a feat!

So come and hear the forest banter,
Where every critter is a planter.
In the shady nooks, tales unfurl,
Under leafy roofs, a laughter whirl.

Secrets of the Shaded Grove

In a glade where shadows play,
Chirping crickets dance and sway.
A fox wears glasses, oh what a sight,
Reading books in the pale moonlight!

The turtles gossip about hat trends,
Claiming boldness with shells that bends.
A snail named Gary thinks he's cool,
He slides through mud, a slippery fool!

A raccoon juggles acorns too,
He's got talent, oh yes it's true!
But drops them all, what a great mess,
He sighs and shrugs, nothing less!

With whispers echoing around the trees,
Nature's jesters spread such ease.
Life's a joke, or so they say,
In this grove where laughter plays.

Echoes of the Enchanted Glade

In the glade where magic springs,
A pixie learns to play with strings.
She strums a tune; it's quite a flop,
But all the gnomes can't stop the bop!

A mushroom tells a silly joke,
While butterflies giggle, and frogs choke.
A lizard dances, tail in tow,
Claiming awards that none would know!

The windy whispers tease the breeze,
While echoes chuckle amongst the trees.
A band of bugs with grand parade,
Step to the rhythm all the way!

So wander here, where laughter's spun,
In secret spots beneath the sun.
The glade is bright with mirthful sights,
And joy erupts in woodland nights.

Shadows Cradled by the Trees

In shadows where the moonlight glows,
A raccoon and rabbit share their woes.
'Why don't we ever catch a break?'
The raccoon sighs, 'For goodness' sake!'

With splashes of laughter in muted tones,
They share their snacks, and even bones.
A lonely owl gives a haughty hoot,
'You both are utterly cute but mute!'

Meanwhile, squirrels plot a heist so sly,
To snatch the seeds as birds fly high.
Their plan is faulty, the trees will see,
As nuts rain down in glorious spree!

So beneath the trees, with giggles found,
Life's a comedy, all around.
For every secret and shadow's plea,
Is a laugh waiting among the leaves.

The Uncharted Whispers

In a nook where squirrels scheme,
Chasing shadows, chasing dreams,
A turtle's tale will make you grin,
With a shell that's clearly lost its spin.

A raccoon wearing a tiny hat,
Trying to sneak in a chat with a cat,
They plot to steal a bowl of cheese,
But both end up stuck in the trees.

The frogs, they laugh with a croaky cheer,
At the antics of critters that seem so dear,
But when the dance party starts to sway,
No one cares how the night turns to day.

So if ever you wander where secrets lie,
Listen closely, don't let a chance go by,
For among the leaves and the playful brawl,
You might just find, you've joined the all!

The Forgotten Echoes of Earth

Beneath the roots, where shadows play,
An old toad croaks, 'This is my day!'
He's got a microphone made of twigs,
Hosting a show of jittery jigs.

The hedgehogs come dressed for the ball,
With paper hats that wobble and sprawl,
They twirl and spin in a frantic dance,
Complaining that life has no second chance.

And why's the fox wearing shoes of blue?
Said it's a fashion from year '92!
It's truly the talk of the animal town,
Even the owls can't keep them down.

So if you hear a cacophony loud,
Of creatures who've gathered, feeling proud,
Join the fun, become part of the lore,
For laughter echoes, forever more!

Dreams Buried in the Underbrush

In the bramble where the giggles reside,
A chipmunk plans a wild joyride,
With nuts as fuel for a speedy quest,
Yet ends up trapped in a sunflower nest.

The bunny's got a map drawn in paste,
But forgets where he's journeying in haste,
He hops over roots and tumbles down,
With every thud, the laughter's renown.

The time flies by like a dragonfly,
While the ants, they march and wonder why,
With tiny drums to keep the beat,
They start a parade that's quite the feat.

So wander through where the funny stops,
And unearth laughter in giggly hops,
For in this glade of whimsical cheer,
Every corner holds a comical year!

Tapestry of the Secretive Woods

In the forest where laughter blooms,
Skunks in tuxedos twist with brooms,
While owls debate the latest fads,
Keeping track of gossipy lads.

Beneath the branches, in a leafy nook,
A family of mice writes a funny book,
With tales of cheese and roller skates,
And mice that dream of glorious plates.

The bears craft hats from springtime flowers,
Claiming they're fashion for all the hours,
With honey drips as their sticky glue,
They strut and stroll like they always knew.

So come along where the quirks unfold,
In playful woods, far from the cold,
For every step has a story to share,
Of giggles and grins, everywhere!

Beneath the Knotted Roots

In a tangle of roots, where the silliness grows,
The mice wear top hats, and the dandelion glows.
A rabbit with glasses sips tea on a leaf,
While the duck, quite dapper, aims for the chief.

The whispers of beetles are filled with delight,
They gossip and chuckle throughout the night.
A snail races past with a grin on its face,
Leaving trails of giggles all over the place.

The hedgehogs play poker, the stakes are quite high,
With acorn-shaped chips, oh my, oh my!
A comical scene where the critters convene,
In a world that is silly and bright and serene.

Beneath every root, there's a party in style,
With critters so merry, they dance for a while.
So if you should wander where laughter is true,
You might just find the roots laughing with you.

The Veil of Verdant Silence

Behind leafy curtains, where secrets are spun,
The toads wear bow ties, and the larks try to run.
With chortles and chirps floating soft on the air,
There's mischief afoot, if you sit in a chair.

The squirrels debate on the best acorn pie,
While the owls hoot laughter beneath the blue sky.
A fox with a beret recites funny lore,
As the badgers clap paws and holler for more.

In bushes of laughter, the shadows take part,
With echoes of chuckles that warm up the heart.
A waltz through the weeds reveals jokes from the past,
Where the tickle of thyme makes good times last.

So venture with glee through this green, joyful mist,
Where each rustle of leaves is a giggle you've missed.
For beneath the leaves, with a whimsical pause,
The veil of laughter is nature's applause.

Where the Ferns Keep Watch

Amongst the tall ferns, quite watchful and sly,
The slugs play charades with a wink in their eye.
A chameleon's game hides a truth or a jest,
While a porcupine plays the zaniest guest.

A hedgehog in disguise fashions wigs from the grass,
While giggling from shadows, they all take a pass.
With each step you take, hear the chuckles grow loud,
It's a giggly gathering, a comical crowd.

The mushrooms jump in just to show off their moves,
With wild fern dancers that all seem to groove.
A critter band plays with a wobbly beat,
As the dance floor of leaves hosts this funny retreat.

The laughter erupts as they twirl and they spin,
With roots like the rhythm, they know how to win.
So, peek through the ferns, there's joy to be found,
In the giggles and grins where the good times abound.

Lost amongst the Verdant Shadows

In the thicket of green, where the shadows do play,
The gnomes tell tall tales of the silliest day.
With hats that are floppy and boots that are tall,
They dance in a circle, oh, having a ball.

The vines twist with laughter, as whispers run wild,
Where the bobbing balloons are a trickster's child.
A raccoon at the center declares he's the king,
While the owl hoots along, sharing jokes on a wing.

The shadows are filled with a jubilant cheer,
As fireflies twinkle with thoughts they hold dear.
The crickets do stand-up, crack jokes without stop,
While the lizards applaud from their sunny top.

So if you feel lost in this magical space,
Just join in the fun and embrace the silliness chase.
For amidst the green shadows, there's mischief galore,
Where laughter and joy can be found evermore.

www.ingramcontent.com/pod-product-compliance
Lightning Source LLC
Chambersburg PA
CBHW071841160426
43209CB00003B/375